Written by David Lambert
Edited by Carol Watson
Illustrated by Bernard Robinson and Ross Wardle

CARNIVAL

# The History of the Dog

Forty million years ago there were small, long-tailed, tree-climbing creatures called *Miacids*. These fierce animals prowled the forests of the land we now know as North America. From the miacids came three groups of descendants:

    *Amphicyon* – wolf-sized bears
    *Borophagus* – hyaena-like creatures
    *Tomarctus* – long-legged foxy dogs

It was the group called *Tomarctus* which led on to all the living breeds of domesticated dogs and to their wild relatives, foxes and wolves.

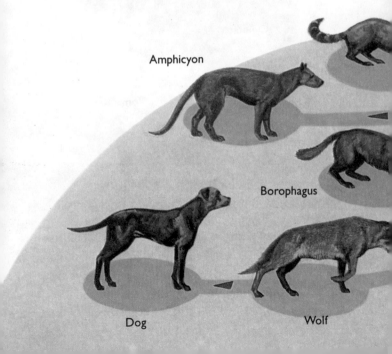

Amphicyon

Borophagus

Dog

Wolf

Some people think that Alsatians, collies, elkhounds, huskies, Samoyeds and terriers all come from northern wolves; while bulldogs, hounds, pointers, setters and mastiffs are descended from Indian wolves.

No-one can be exactly sure how dogs evolved, but fossil bones show that dogs were helping human hunters as long as 10,000 years ago. So dogs have been a friend of man from the time of the Middle Stone Age.

This family tree shows how dogs, wolves, foxes and wild dogs descended from carnivores that lived millions of years ago.

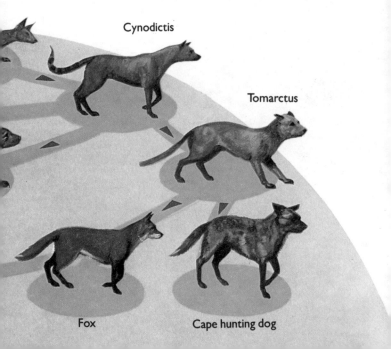

Cynodictis

Tomarctus

Fox

Cape hunting dog

# What is a Dog?

Dogs can be companions, workers, guards, guides or just friends. There are an amazing variety of sizes and shapes – from tiny fluffy things no bigger than a pigeon to huge sleek animals about the height of a four-year old child.

Some dogs belong to a certain breed. This means that their parents were both the same kind of dog. Others have parents of different breeds, and are called crossbreeds. There are hundreds of different breeds but some are neither thoroughbred nor crossbred. These dogs, whose parents are of mixed breeds, are called mongrels.

These dogs are mongrels because their parents were not the offspring of pedigree dogs. Some people think mongrels are stronger and more friendly than thoroughbred dogs.

# A Dog's Body

Although they vary in appearance all dogs share the same body plan. Each animal has the same number of bones. They all have 42 sharp teeth for tearing meat. A dog walks on toes tipped with blunt claws. Its outer coat keeps it dry and its undercoat keeps it warm. When a dog feels too hot it cools itself by panting, because, unlike us, it cannot sweat.

**Features which characterize a dog's breed are:**
1. Shape
2. Size and colour
3. Type of ears and tail
4. Type of coat

From Chihuahua to Labrador, the parts of the dog are the same. A slim, long-legged dog is described as 'racy'; a short, compact dog is known as 'cobby'. The height is always measured from the shoulder.

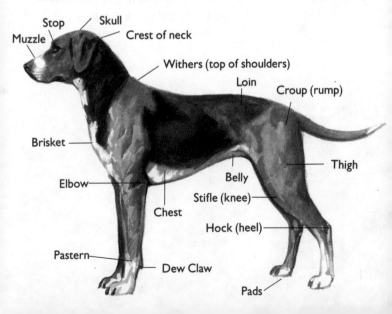

button    pricked    bat

semi-pricked    rose    pendant

Six different types of ear.

In Europe and the United States, there are organizations called Kennel Clubs. These classify dogs into particular groups. In Britain the groups are: Hound, Gundog, Toy, Terrier, Utility and Working dog.

Different types of tail.
Dogs of certain breeds
have their tails docked
while they are puppies.

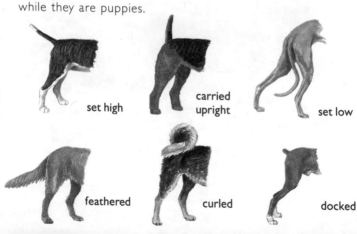

set high    carried upright    set low

feathered    curled    docked

# Helpful Dogs

Certain breeds of dog are so intelligent and trust-
worthy they can be used to help us. They can be
trained to guide blind people around obstacles and
through city streets. These dogs even disobey orders that might lead their owners into danger.

Because dogs have a keener sense of smell and
hearing than us, they can often do certain tasks
better than we can. They are able to sniff out explosives or harmful drugs – and they can track down
lost people, stolen goods or the thieves who stole
them.

A guide dog leads its blind
master through a busy town.

A police dog sniffs travellers suitcases. Its trained nose can detect explosives or drugs that may be lying hidden inside.

Many people have been saved from drowning by dogs, who even if they cannot swim to the rescue, will run to alert those who can. Dogs are also used to track down people who are buried in earthquakes or avalanches.

Each year scientists use thousands of dogs in research experiments – the most famous of all was the dog who became the world's first traveller in space.

Laika, a terrier from Russia, was the first animal in space.

A trained dog digs in the snow for an avalanche victim who has been tracked down by the dog's keen sense of smell.

# Working Dogs

## Shepherd Dogs

At one time, dogs had to hunt for their food, chasing wild animals and following herds. Gradually, over the years, people have bred dogs that will chase other animals, but not harm them. Farmers use these kinds of dog to guard and round up their flocks and herds.

A team of Border Collies, trained to work together, drive sheep into a pen, obeying the orders whistled by the shepherd.

Rough Collie

Smooth Collie

Bearded Collie

Border Collie

Many years ago there were dogs who used to round up *colleys* – the nimble, black-faced sheep that roamed the mountains of Scotland. The descendants of these dogs are the Collies we know today. The most intelligent and trainable of all is the Border Collie, which is medium-sized and usually black and white.

## German Shepherd

The German Shepherd, or Alsatian dog, has been used as a guard for animals and property since man was a hunter. Nowadays they are most often used as police or guard dogs. These animals are tough, intelligent, alert and well-disciplined. Although they look very wolf-like, Alsatians are no more closely related to wolves than any other dogs.

## Briard

## Old English Sheepdog

The Briard is a dog which used to guard the sheep flocks of Brie in France, but nowadays it is more often a family pet.

The Komondor and the Old English Sheepdog are shepherd dogs with very thick, long coats which were bred to keep the dogs warm in the wintry weather. Their coats are so long their eyes are usually hidden.

**Maremma**

**Puli**

The beautiful, big Maremma with its long, white coat was bred in Italy to guard flocks against bears, wolves and thieves.

It is very important for a sheepdog to be obedient. Unruly dogs can frighten the sheep and waste time. The little Kelpie, which comes from Australia, is so highly disciplined when trained, it can jump on or over the backs of sheep without worrying them. Pulis, from Hungary, can also learn this skill.

Corgis and their relatives, the Västgötaspets were bred as cattle herders. They used to nip the cows' heels to drive them to market.

**Kelpie**

# Friend to Travellers

There are some places in the world where man could not go without the help of his friend, the dog.

**St Bernard**

Crossing the mountains of Switzerland can often be difficult and dangerous. As long ago as the 17th century the monks of St Bernard de Menthon kept and bred dogs to guide and rescue travellers from the snowdrifts of the Swiss Alps. These dogs were the ancestors of the St Bernard we know today.

**Newfoundland**

The Newfoundland was used to help trappers in the snowy North American wastes. Although very large dogs, they are gentle and make good pets. Newfoundlands are powerful swimmers and sometimes rescue drowning people. It is said that their ancestors were taken to Canada by French fishermen, which is maybe why they feel at home in the water.

**Pyrenean Mountain Dog**

**Bernese Mountain Dog**

The Pyrenean Mountain Dog has been used both as a guard dog and a sheep dog, and nowadays is sometimes used as a pack animal.

For centuries Siberian Huskies and Samoyeds pulled the sleds of Siberian nomads, herded their reindeer and guarded their tents. These brave and sturdy dogs are still used in the far north and on polar expeditions for hauling laden sledges over ice and snow. The Alaskan Malamute can cover more than 80 kilometres a day dragging the weight of four men. All these three breeds make friendly pets, but not surprisingly need a lot of exercise.

# Guard Dogs

Guard dogs, like sheepdogs, need to be loyal, obedient, strong and courageous. In the 19th century a tax collector, called Louis Dobermann, used local dogs to breed an animal that would guard the money he carried. The result was the Dobermann Pinscher, a fine dog which is proud, elegant, fast and fearless. No breed makes a better watchdog or police dog.

Two German dogs, the Rottweiler and the Boxer also make powerful bodyguards. Rottweilers were originally used to protect herds of cattle but nowadays are trained in police and mountain rescue work. Boxers are mastiffs, once used to hunt bears and guard cattle. Now they are used as fearsome watchdogs.

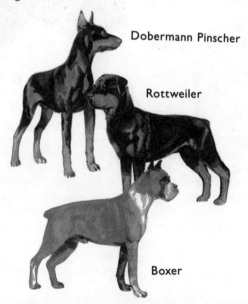

Dobermann Pinscher

Rottweiler

Boxer

Police dogs are trained to attack and seize the enemy. Padding protects the 'victim' from the dogs' fangs.

**Tibetan Mastiff**

**Mastiff**

# Dogs at War

Dogs are carnivores (meat eaters) and so they have an instinct for hunting and killing. This instinct not only makes them brilliant guard dogs, but also means they can be trained to fight for their masters as well as themselves.

In ancient times soldiers took fierce dogs into battle to attack the enemy. Over two thousand years

A war-dog from the Middle Ages.

Bull Terrier

Bulldog

ago the Greek Molossi tribe bred a war-dog to unleash on the Persians. This dog was like a mastiff and was called a Molossus.

In the Middle Ages dogs were given armour. They charged into battle wearing suits of leather with sharp spikes jutting over their heads and pots of flaming sulphur and resin strapped to their backs. The mounted knights of the enemy would be thrown from their horses as the animals reared up in terror.

In later years man bred dogs to fight and bait bulls for cruel sport. These dogs were the ancestors of the Bull Terrier, Staffordshire Bull Terrier and the Bulldog.

In modern times, dogs have also been used during wartime. In World War II more than 10,000 dogs served with the Allied forces. Under fire, they carried messages and medical supplies, and helped to find wounded soldiers among those left for dead on the battlefield.

# Gundogs

Man first made friends with the dog in order to have help with his hunting. The dog could find the prey, while the man could kill it more efficiently. If the man killed a large animal there was some spare for the dog. So the friendship between them grew.

Springer Spaniel

Springer spaniels scare, or 'spring' birds into the air and fetch them when they are shot.

Modern 'sporting' breeds include pointers, setters, spaniels and retrievers. **Each breed has a special way of hunting:**
1. When a *pointer* finds a hare or game bird it stands still with its head, body and tail pointed like an arrow towards the quarry.

2. *Setters* crouch, or 'set' in the same way.
3. *Spaniels* flush out game from grass and shrubs.
4. *Retrievers* also fetch dead game birds. These are active, powerful dogs, larger than spaniels, but gentle enough to carry an egg in their jaws.

# Spaniels

Most spaniels have sturdy bodies, silky coats, long floppy ears, big eyes and dome-shaped skulls. Their colours and sizes vary greatly.

American Cocker Spaniel

Clumber Spaniel

Cocker Spaniel

# Pointers and Setters

Setters are very elegant dogs with silky coats and feathered legs and tails. English setters are white with markings of black, lemon, liver or black-and-tan. The Irish setter (Red Setter) has a flat chestnut coat. The largest and heaviest of the setters is the Scottish Gordon setter. All setters make lovable pets but they do need a lot of exercise.

English Setter

Irish Setter

Gordon Setter

# Retrievers

Golden Retriever

The most popular retriever is the Labrador which has a short, dense, black or yellow coat. They make good-tempered pets, police retrieval dogs and guide dogs for the blind.

Labrador Retriever

Flat-coated Retriever

Cheseapeake Bay Retreiver

# Terriers

The word terrier comes from *terra* – the Latin word for earth. These dogs are given this name because they were bred to dig out rats, rabbits, foxes or badgers from their holes. Modern terriers come from two main groups: short-legged terriers that could crawl easily inside burrows; and longer-legged terriers that

Cairn Terrier
Height 24-26cm

Bedlington Terrier
Height 38-41cm

Scottish Terrier
Height 25-28cm

West Highland White Terrier
Height 25-28cm

Sealyham Terrier
Height 26-35cm

Dandie Dinmont Terrie
Height 20-28cm

Skye Terrier
Height 24-25cm

could run fast and dig, but were too big to squeeze into a burrow.

Most terriers are small, hardy British breeds with hard or wiry hair. They come in a variety of shapes and sizes.

Of the long-legged breeds, the wiry-coated, black and tan Airedale is the largest. It is a good hunter and is often used by the police and the army, as is the Irish terrier.

Norfolk Terrier
Height 23-25cm

Norwich Terrier
Height 22-25cm

Border Terrier
Height 26-30cm

Manchester Terrier
Height 38-41cm

Australian Terrier
Height 24-25cm

Staffordshire Bull Terrier
Height 35-40cm

Yorkshire Terrier
Hieght 18-20cm

Miniature Schnauzer
Height 33-35cm

# Hounds

Since ancient times hounds have been bred to hunt with man. They are incredibly fast, have great stamina and a keen sense of smell. Hounds are divided into two groups:
1. Those that track down their prey by scent.
2. Those that sight and then run after their victim.
Nowadays it is those from the second group which are used for competitive sports.

The oldest known hounds come from Ancient Egypt and Arabia. The hound was the favoured friend of the Pharoahs. The Pharoah Hound of today looks very like the dog-headed Egyptian god, Anubis.

The Whippet is more a modern breed. It is less expensive to buy than a greyhound and is a popular racing dog.

Pharoah Hound

Whippet

Greyhound

## Sight Hounds

The tall, graceful Borzoi and the Afghan are the most elegant of the sight hounds. The Russians used to keep Borzois for hunting wolves, rabbits and hares. They were said 'to run as fast as the wind'. Afghans were once used to hunt deer and guard sheep in the rugged hills of their native land.

**Afghan Hound**

**Irish Wolfhound**

**Deerhound**

The Deerhound and Irish wolfhound are more rugged, and amongst the tallest of dogs. The Deerhound was used to hunt red deer, and the Wolfhound to hunt wolves.

# Scent Hounds

Bloodhound

Scent hounds are usually sturdy with broad noses. They can track their prey by its scent for hours. When they reach their quarry they either attack it, or trap it until the huntsman arrives.

The Bloodhound is the oldest of all scent hounds. It is strong, with drooping ears and loose wrinkled

Dachshund

Dachshunds or 'sausage dogs' were bred to squeeze down badger sets. There are many different kinds of dachshund, some wirehaired; others smoothhaired or longhaired.

skin on the head. This hound is the only one bred especially to hunt humans, but although they are good at seeking out their victim, they are not tough enough to hold onto them. Because of this they are rarely used by the police.

### Basset Hound

Basset Hounds are also sausage shaped, with short legs and large heads like a Bloodhound's. They come from France and were trained to hunt in packs.

Foxhounds, Harriers and Beagles hunt in packs for foxes and hares. Their short, smooth coats are often white with black-and-tan markings. They have hanging ears and long tails carried high.

### Foxhound

# A Dog of Your Own

Most of the dogs in this book can be kept as pets if you have room for them in your home. However, before you get a puppy you must think carefully about what it involves. Dogs need to be fed and exercised regularly – they like company and do not like to be left alone for long periods of time. You need to think about what will happen to your dog when you go away on holiday. Who will look after it? Can you afford to put it in Boarding Kennels?

## Choosing a Puppy

If you decide to buy a puppy, always choose one that is lively, with bright eyes, a clean coat and clean ears. Avoid breeds which you know have lots of ailments. Ask your vet to check it over before making a final decision.

Feed dry food, canned meat or meat and biscuits. You will need less dry food than other kinds of food, but moisten it. Always have a bowl of fresh water nearby.

# Caring for your pet

Give your puppy its own bed or rug to lie on in a quiet place away from draughts. Make sure it always has a bowl of fresh drinking water nearby. Ask your vet exactly what to feed your particular puppy – big dogs may need seven times as much food as small ones. Do not feed them snacks in between meals.

Dogs need things to chew. Give your puppy cowhide strips, a big bone, or other chewy toys, but not bones which are thin enough to splinter or any object which is small enough to swallow.

# Grooming

Most dogs need to have a bath about once a month, but shorthaired dogs need brushing weekly. A longhaired dog may need a daily brush and comb, so make sure you have time to spare before you buy one of these.

# Training

Your puppy will need to be housetrained. This should begin as soon as you get home. Spread out old newspaper on your kitchen floor, and when your pup has eaten, place it on the newspaper. Praise the puppy for using the paper and scold it when it doesn't. Gradually move the paper nearer to the outside door, then eventually into the garden.

As your puppy grows older, teach it to obey simple instructions such as 'sit', 'come' and 'no'. Give it a collar and lead and teach it to walk properly on the lead. Always make sure you have authority in your voice when you speak to it.

# Some Favourite Pets

Miniature Poodle

Japanese Spaniel

Cavalier King Charles Spaniel

**Carnival**
An imprint of the Children's Division
of the Collins Publishing Group
8 Grafton Street, London WIX 3LA

First published by Granada Publishing 1982.
Published in this abridged edition by Carnival 1989.

Illustrations copyright © Granada 1982.

Text copyright © William Collins Sons & Co Ltd 1989

ISBN 0 00 194953 5

Printed & bound in Great Britain by
BPCC Paulton Books Limited

Cover illustration by Peter Stevenson

A catalogue record for this book is available from the
British Library

This book was first published by Ladybird Books as
*Old King Cole and other nursery rhymes*

Published by Ladybird Books Ltd    Loughborough
Leicestershire    UK
Ladybird Books Inc    Auburn    Maine    04210    USA

Printed in England

© LADYBIRD BOOKS LTD MCMLXXXIV

# My first nursery rhymes

Illustrated by Ken McKie

Ladybird Books

Old King Cole

Was a merry old soul,

And a merry old soul was he;

He called for his pipe,

And he called for his bowl,

And he called for his fiddlers three.

Hickory, dickory, dock,
The mouse ran up the clock.
The clock struck one,
The mouse was gone,
Hickory, dickory, dock.

Georgie Porgie,
pudding and pie,
Kissed the girls
and made them cry;
When the boys came
out to play,
Georgie Porgie ran away.

Little Miss Muffet
Sat on a tuffet,
Eating her curds and whey;
There came a big spider,
Who sat down beside her
And frightened Miss Muffet away.

Diddle, diddle, dumpling,
	my son John,
Went to bed
	with his trousers on;
One shoe off
	and the other shoe on,
Diddle, diddle, dumpling,
	my son John.

Hush-a-bye, baby,
          on the tree top,

When the wind blows
          the cradle will rock;

When the bough breaks,
          the cradle will fall,

Down will come baby,
          cradle and all.

Pease porridge hot,
Pease porridge cold,
Pease porridge in the pot,
    Nine days old.

Some like it hot,
Some like it cold,
Some like it in the pot,
    Nine days old.

Little Tommy Tucker,
Sings for his supper:
What shall we give him?
White bread and butter.
How will he cut it
Without a knife?
How will he marry
Without a wife?

Ride a cock-horse
       to Banbury Cross,
To see a fine lady
       upon a white horse;
Rings on her fingers
       and bells on her toes,
She shall have music
       wherever she goes.

Tom, Tom, the piper's son,
Stole a pig and away did run;
The pig was eat
And Tom was bea
And Tom went howling down
the street.

Hot cross buns!
Hot cross buns!
One a penny, two a penny,
Hot cross buns!
If you have no daughters,
Give them to your sons,
One a penny, two a penny,
Hot cross buns!

Mary, Mary, quite contrary,
How does your garden grow?
With silver bells and cockle shells
And pretty maids all in a row.

Yankee Doodle came to town,
Riding on a pony;
He stuck a feather in his cap
And called it macaroni.

Jack Sprat could eat no fat,
His wife could eat no lean,
And so between them both, you see,
They licked the platter clean.

Doctor Foster went to Gloucester
In a shower of rain;
He stepped in a puddle,
Right up to his middle,
And never went there again.

Old Mother Hubbard
Went to the cupboard,
To get her poor dog a bone;
But when she got there
The cupboard was bare
And so the poor dog had none.

Higgledy Piggledy, my black hen,
She lays eggs for gentlemen;
Sometimes nine and sometimes ten
Higgledy, Piggledy, my black hen.

The Queen of Hearts
She made some tarts,
All on a summer's day;
The Knave of Hearts
He stole the tarts,
And took them right away.

The King of Hearts,
Called for the tarts,
And beat the Knave full sore;
The Knave of Hearts
Brought back the tarts,
And vowed he'd steal no more.

Rub-a-dub-dub,
Three men in a tub,
And how do you think
             they got there?
The butcher, the baker,
The candlestick-maker,
They all jumped out of a
             rotten potato,
'Twas enough to make a man stare.

Curly-locks, Curly-locks,
Wilt thou be mine?
Thou shalt not wash dishes
Nor yet feed the swine,
But sit on a cushion
And sew a fine seam,
And feed upon strawberries,
Sugar and cream.